I Like This Heart Space

Quotations & Reflections
to Inspire Your Best Self

I Like This Heart Space

Quotations & Reflections to Inspire Your Best Self

A *Gentle & Kind* Book

SUZI LARKIN, M.A.

This book contains advice relating to personal well-being. This book is designed to provide accurate information about the subject matter and all efforts have been made to assure the accuracy at time of publication. However, the information, ideas, and suggestions in this book are not intended as a substitute for consultation with health-care or mental health professionals. If you require such assistance, seek the services of a mental health or other healthcare professional.

I Like This Heart Space: Quotations & Reflections to Inspire Your Best Self

ISBN: 9798376297001

Independently Published

SuziLarkin.com

Dedicated to

*the light that is within
each of us.*

CONTENTS

INTRODUCTION

**I like this place and could
willingly waste my time in it.**

William Shakespeare

AS YOU LIKE IT, CELIA ACT II, 4, 812

Whatever you are seeking, I invite you to open this book to a random page and read the quotation and my – hopefully not too random – thoughts on it. I want it to be a place that you'd like to spend time refreshing your spirit, examining your mind-set, connecting with your heart.

I Like This Heart Space: Quotations & Reflections to Inspire Your Best Self is like having a conversation with a good friend; I invite you to willingly waste your time inside the pages.

Pick up this book to experience some encouragement, laughter, perspective, or motivation to be the best version of yourself, to have faith in yourself. Cast aside your limiting beliefs. Gain insight into your perceived obstacles. Be reminded of who you are. Gently invite yourself to become your best self.

Whether you read one each day, an entire section in one sitting, or just jump around, you can return to these quotations and reflections again and again; you will discover fresh insights and inspiration to create the life you want – to follow your dreams.

balance
create
nurture

Chapter 1

LIFE

How should we live our lives?

Live your life from your heart; live a balanced life. For every exhale, there is an inhale. Your life is balanced.

You create your life. You decide who you are and what you'll do in this world. We experience less stress when life is in balance. For every worry, there is an answer, an end to anxious anticipation. For every need, there is nurture. For every beginning, there is an ending. For every ending, there is a beginning.

Some prescriptions for life.

Life is a balance of holding on and letting go.

Rumi

Rumi's prescription for achieving balance is a good one to keep coming back to. Come back to it when your life feels overwhelming, stressful, sad, or tired. The two concepts of holding on and letting go are monumental – yet seem on the surface to be obvious and simple. Getting good at both holding on and letting go brings the serenity of balance.

Holding on is valued in society: *hold your temper, hold on to what you have, hold on to your dreams, hold your horses, hold that thought, hold your loved ones close, hold onto your convictions, take hold of yourself, get a grip. How are you holding up?* And don't get me started on all the admonitions to *hang on.* Yes, we need to hold on and we also need to learn how to let go. When your first pet dies, you learn to let go; it takes a long time, but you learn how to cope with the loss. When you are angry, you learn how to let it go and forgive (yourself and the other person involved).

When you have children, you learn that life is about letting go: their first steps and their first trip away from you, and when they leave the nest after high school or college. When my adult daughters come home to visit for the holidays, it is definitely an exercise in holding on and letting go. I cherish the time we have together and I try to hold on to it while it lasts. A few days later when they leave, I need to let go.

**Life isn't about finding yourself.
Life is about creating yourself.**

George Bernard Shaw

Have the confidence and courage to create the version of yourself you know in your heart you wish to be. Pay attention to yourself: learn who you are and who you want to be. You are that person!

You are many versions of your "self." Choose which one you want to be the most often; choose who you need to be at work, at school, at home. Observe how they merge over the years.

Hone your skills, develop your character. Keep on learning, keep on creating yourself. Create the best version of yourself and have the courage to share your wonderful self with the world.

**What is important in life is life,
and not the result of life.**

Johann Wolfgang von Goethe

If we're evaluating how our lives are going, we want to remember: focus on your efforts, and not on the results. I'm reminded of the saying: *It's not how many days in your life that is important, but the amount of life in your days.* While we cannot all live each day as if it were our last and take off on a vacation, (we have jobs, kids, mortgages, etc.) we *can* do one small thing that brings joy to someone, or to our own lives. Something as easy and simple as a smile will spread cheer and generate warm feelings.

When you do your best to love yourself and others, you are giving the best efforts that anyone could ask for in this life. No need to worry about the results, they will be amazing.

Learn from yesterday, live for today and hope for tomorrow.

Albert Einstein

Learning from past mistakes and successes helps us to live a better life today. Envisioning a better tomorrow can spark enthusiasm and motivation in our current tasks and relationships.

Einstein speaks to me about balance in this quotation because he combines learning and living, and he balances them with the time we have. We only have the present to live in, so he says live for today. Our past experiences can shape the way we choose to live our lives in the present, so he advises us to learn from yesterday, without trying to stay rooted in the past. While living in the present, we are able to hope and dream and lay groundwork for the future. Life in balance.

Are you living in the past? Maybe, just for a moment, you can choose to focus on the present and tap into hope. What are your dreams and goals? Take small intentional steps today. Begin to create the life you desire.

People spend most of their lives worrying about things that never happen.

Moliere

Spend your time wisely; don't spend it worrying about things that probably won't happen. Think about something that you were worried about that did *not* happen. Got it? Now, feel the relief. Whew. Exhale. I'm so glad THAT didn't happen! Catch yourself next time you are worrying and try to talk yourself out of it. Look up actuarial tables if you must, but talk yourself out of the likelihood that the bad thing will happen.

Many of us suffer from anxiety – and that is real – so we are good friends with worry. There are ways to balance out the amount of energy you spend feeling anxious and worrying though. To counteract the un-invited worries and generalized anxiety, you can try: meditation, yoga, deep breathing, running, dancing, acting, singing, or any other activities that will take your mind's focus and your body's energy *off worry* and *shift it on to* an activity that will boost your energy rather than drain it.

And… breathe. You've got this.

The purpose of life is to live it, to taste experience to the utmost, to reach out eagerly and without fear for newer and richer experience.

Eleanor Roosevelt

Taste experience to the utmost. Reach out eagerly without fear. Live your life to its fullest. Go for it. Follow your dreams. Stay awake and focus on the present moment while reaching toward your future. This is your best life.

You'll find new experiences to enrich your life. You'll find a life worth living.

It's your life – it's the only one you have. Live it well.

The art of knowing is knowing what to ignore.

Rumi

Focus on the good – the good in you and the good in others. Ignore attempts to suck you into darkness and shame.

You are not who or what someone else says you are. You know what is true and what to ignore. Consult your center, your heart, your soul and follow the path of right, not wrong. Ignore destructive comments and ignore toxic people who need to tear you down to feel good about themselves.

Stay as far away as you can when people are throwing shame. Ignore them. Ignore their words. When they heal their own wounds, they will not need to shame you. For now, just ignore them.

Every moment is
a fresh beginning.

T.S. Eliot

In *Anne of Green Gables*, Anne Shirley says that each day is new, with no mistakes in it. I agree! Each day *is* a new opportunity. Each day is a *beginning*.

Choose what you want to do with your fresh beginnings. There is so much freedom in them! The possibilities are awe inspiring.

**When you rise in the morning,
give thanks for the light, for your life,
for your strength.**

Tecumseh

Give thanks.

Rise and give thanks for the light outside your bed-room curtain this morning. It came! A new morning! No matter how difficult the night is, morning always follows.

Rise and give thanks for your life this morning. You are here! You are alive! You are the embodiment of possibility!

Rise and give thanks for your strength this morning. You made it through the night! You have survived your past and gained strength. Your inner strength and your physical strength – however much you have – are still here. You are strong.

Now take a moment to think of all the people you are

grateful for this morning. Now think of all the people who are grateful that *you are here* this morning.

Give thanks.

be bold
take risks
be free

Chapter 2

COURAGE

To Be Different, Be Vulnerable,
Be You, Take Risks

Courage: The quality of mind or spirit that enables
you to face difficulty, danger, pain, and more.

**Be who you were created to be,
and you will set the world on fire.**

St. Catherine of Sienna

Do you know who you were created to be? Do you know who you are? Knowing and accepting yourself is foundational, fundamental to being your best self and living your best life.

This is your invitation to explore, to explore who you are and share your gifts with the world. Sounds simple, doesn't it? We know it is not as easy as it seems.

What makes this hard? Maybe you have been criticized too often to share who you are with more than a small circle of friends and family. Maybe you've been ignored when you tried to share your true self.

It's okay to be cautious, but the more you share of yourself with the world, the richer your experience of life will be. It's like the pebble in the pond. You drop it in and it creates ripples – circle after circle, the vibration touches every molecule of the pond as it spreads outward. You never know when that vibration will touch someone else's life, someone else's ripple.

Knowing who you are, accepting who you are, and living your life from that place—it all creates energy. Use that energy to set the world on fire with your creativity, your intentionality, your ideas, and your love.

Start with knowing who you are, then take courage to BE who you are out in the world.

Boldness be my friend.

William Shakespeare

How often do you wish that you had a friend – right there beside you – when you felt nervous, tentative or hesitant? Shakespeare's use of the word "friend," makes me feel like I'm not alone. I feel that I can call on a part of myself – my boldness – to be with me, to be my friend.

Your inner courage is your friend. Visit often.

Avoiding danger is no safer in the long run than outright exposure. The fearful are caught as often as the bold. Faith alone defends. Life is either a daring adventure or nothing. To keep our faces toward change and behave like free spirits in the presence of fate is strength undefeatable.

Helen Keller

I want a daring adventure, I do! But I want to be safe and avoid danger. I'm not going to go jump off a cliff. I know, I know, a lot of people jump off cliffs into the water below and they are fine and that is a great daring adventure for *them*, but it's not my cup of tea.

A daring adventure for me might involve travel or pursuing a goal that I am not sure I can reach, whether personal or professional. Simply trying something new or making a new friend can be a daring adventure. This is when we need to have faith in ourselves and take a risk. The fear of rejection when we take a risk and meet new people and make new friends is right up there with public speaking for many people.

Today, face change and behave like a free spirit – you'll find your strength there!

**Are you in earnest? Seize this very minute–
What you can do, or dream you can, begin it,
Boldness has genius, power, and magic in it,
Only engage, and then the mind grows heated—
Begin it, and the work will be completed!**

Faust by Johann Wolfgang von Goethe

TRANSLATED BY JOHN ANSTER, 1835

Be bold! Start now! If you have a desire, an idea, a dream then you must be bold and begin it. Take small steps, but *do take steps*. Be bold, have courage, and begin because, "boldness has genius, power, and magic in it." Yes! You have genius in you.

But you must start: "Only engage, and then the mind grows heated…" Showing up, or starting is the hardest part. You can do it. You can, because once you start, your mind and your entire being can become engaged and you will be *doing* it, instead of thinking about doing it. "Begin it, and the work will be completed!" Yes! This is you. You can do this. The hardest part is the start. Your boldness to begin has magic in it.

The best protection any woman can have is courage.

Elizabeth Cady Stanton

Back in the 19th century when suffragette Elizabeth Cady Stanton lived, women were generally thought to need "protection." What did they need protection from? Well, quite often it was from men. Ironically, it was much more acceptable at that time for men to be abusive or violent to their wives and daughters because women were considered to be their property. Too often, women actually needed protection from the men closest to them.

Men sought to protect women from anything that they thought would be upsetting. For example, they sought to protect women from carriages going too fast in the streets. They even wanted to "protect" women from certain ideas and knowledge about the world.

What can protect us, save us from fear, doubt, harm,

difficulty? Courage is one antidote. Courage can protect us, whether it is 1850 or 2023.

Common knowledge tells us that when we have the courage to face our fears, our fears often disappear. Or, if they don't disappear, we tame them and we do not allow them to paralyze us any longer. We can live with our old fears and move forward with courage.

Courage is your new friend. Courage is you. Courage is your frame of mind when you do not overthink. Courage is when you believe in yourself. Listen to that voice inside you that says, "I can do this. I am afraid and nervous but I have looked at this situation or task and I can ask my fear to stand aside while my courage leads me forward."

Have faith in yourself. This is courage. This is you.

**It's not because things are difficult
that we dare not venture.
It's because we dare not venture
that they are difficult.**

Seneca

What a reverse in ordinary thinking! Here we are, thinking that we can't attempt something because it seems too difficult or scary, only to discover that it is not that difficult or scary once we attempt it. It is not scary, but thinking makes it so.

I know more than one person who has said, "I could never be in a play, it's too scary and it would be difficult to memorize all those lines." I also know that these very same people have auditioned for a community theatre play and thoroughly enjoyed it acting in it! And they did memorize all those lines.
So, it is really another case of you being your own obstacle, or your thoughts being obstacles.

Feel the fear and do it anyway. You alone know what you can do when you dare to venture forth.

**Take risks in your life,
if you win, you can lead,
if you lose, you can guide.**

Swami Vivekananda

Did you laugh when you read this one? I did. At first this seems almost like a joke, doesn't it? Using humor to impart wisdom creates a heightened response, so I might remember it longer than a wise quotation that is not funny. What a great way to remind us of this fact: when people make mistakes, the outcome is productive. We learn so much from our mistakes that we can actually teach others how to succeed!

Making mistakes means we are taking risks, and taking risks can help us to gain wisdom.

Twenty years from now you will be
more disappointed by the things that
you didn't do than by the ones you
did do. So throw off the bowlines.
Sail away from the safe harbor.
Catch the trade winds in your sails.
Explore – Dream – Discover.

Mark Twain

Have courage! Taking risks now will save you from regret later. Explore! Dream! Discover! The world is just outside your doorstep. What will you find?

Follow your path, and
let the people talk.

Dante

Focus on your path, not on what anyone else thinks of you and your journey. You do not need to succumb to the pressure to conform.

Don't worry about what others think and say about you! Be true to your values and be true to yourself.

change
explore
integrity

Chapter 3

DISCOVER

Define Your Character,
Delight in Yourself

Discover yourself by taking a look at who you are and who you decide to be each day. What do your actions say about who you are? In many ways, your actions define you. Your character develops throughout your life and is shaped by your actions.

And give yourself permission to delight in yourself each day. Discover how *delightful* you are and you'll soon discover the *delightfulness* of those around you.

Our deeds determine us, as much as we determine our deeds.

George Eliot

What we do each day forms our character as much as our character determines what we do. The good that we do shows up in our character. The same can be said for negative character traits, so it's a good idea to remember the effect your deeds have.

What deeds are we talking about? If you hold the door open for someone, if you let someone go in front of you in line at the store, if you say thank you to someone who held the door open for you, if you offer to listen to the full story of a friend who is upset or joyful, all those deeds show you to be thoughtful, considerate, kind, grateful, patient, loving, and more. Those are character traits you own. Those traits are ways others would use to describe you.

Another way to say this is: You determine what you do, and what you do determines you.

**A person without a sense of humor is
like a wagon without springs.
It's jolted by every pebble on the road.**

Henry Ward Beecher

How is your wagon built? I know that I had a good sense of humor once, but life has worn me down lately so that even I judge myself as too serious, too earnest. The pandemic was a difficult and sad time for so many people. We got through it but life has changed.

Still, we move on. I went on a walk through the snowy streets a day or two before New Year's Eve with one of my best friends, and we laughed. We laughed more than once! It was so refreshing to be able to laugh about our usual concerns and how we usually handle them. We discussed the ways in which we talk about our struggles with friends and close family members, and this gave each of us a new perspective – and the freedom to find the humor in how we handle life's struggles.

Resilience. We found ourselves to be resilient. And I realized that my sense of humor *is* intact, it was just pushed deep down inside me. Like a Genie let out of the bottle, my sense of humor is free. I'm happy to not be jolted by every pebble or bump in the road, because if there is one thing in life we can count on in Minnesota, it is potholes in the roads.

> **Our greatest ability as humans
> is not to change the world;
> but to change ourselves.**
>
> *Mahatma Gandhi*

This notion of change is so powerful because when your project is to change yourself, you don't need to enroll anyone else in your idea of what you'd like to do.

Our greatest ability is to change ourselves. We have that ability. We can change part of our character or we can even just make a small change like acquiring a new habit. When we use our ability to change, we can have a huge impact on others in our lives and therefore in the world.

In the 1990's, doing "random acts of kindness," was popular. People did small things like pay for the person's meal behind them at the fast-food drive through, or let someone cut in front of them on the freeway or in a grocery store line. More and more people started doing more and more random acts of kindness. The result was that this single behavior change – to perform a random act of kindness for someone – changed our world into a better place.

Change one thing that you do and you can change the world.

The only person you are destined to become is the person you decide to be.

Ralph Waldo Emerson

Are you who you are because you consciously decided to be that way? So many factors influence our character, and we are not always aware of all of them. Certainly, where you were born, who your parents and family were and how they interacted with you had an impact on the person you are today, so did your teachers and friends along the way. And life experiences also helped form your character.

Who is it that you decided to be and when did you make those decisions? Are you quiet, loud, ambitious, kind, funny, bold, tough, gentle, smart, helpful, adventurous?

Do your decisions about who you decided to be still serve you today? Reflecting on these questions will help you clarify your next goals, your next adventure.

Just know that you can always make a new decision each day.

**To do good things in the world,
first you must know who you are and
what gives meaning to your life.**

Robert Browning

What gives meaning to your life? For me, it is helping people. I used to teach public speaking and coach
a college speech team. Later, I found a career in human resources (mostly recruiting and hiring people).
These jobs gave me an opportunity to help others and
I enjoyed the work immensely. Then, when I had my
daughters, I became a Home Educator or a Home
School Mom and that was the best job ever. I think all
parents home-school their kids in some part because
they are their child's first teacher. I just made it my
career. It was a good career decision for me.

Nothing was more meaningful than being given the
honor of being their mom and the privilege of staying home with them to teach them and learn about
them while my husband went to his office each day.
At that point in my life, I did finally know who I was

and what gave meaning to my life. And I'd like to say that *I did* "do good things in the world," as Robert Browning said. I loved helping them learn, especially to read. And watching as my child made science discoveries or discovered rules of grammar was an amazing experience!

As any educator (or mom or dad) knows, your work is meaningful and good when you help someone learn. It can be learning a concept or a skill, or learning how to achieve a goal – even a goal as fundamental as learning to tie your shoes or ride a bicycle. Those are meaningful experiences filled with joy and you can see that exuberance on their faces.

Knowing who you are and what gives meaning to your life is a wonderful life-long process. And I am confident that you will do many good things in the world.

**If you don't know, ask. You will be a
fool for the moment, but a wise man
for the rest of your life.**

Seneca

People who ask questions are brave. Let's face it: there
is always a chance that you will annoy someone by
asking them a question. This ancient quotation reminds us that if we take that small risk of irritating
someone or appearing foolish, we will gain not only
knowledge, but confidence.

This is one of those practices that you'll hear referred
to as "character building." And it is. If you make a
practice, or habit, of asking questions when you don't
know, it will get easier. And you will become wise.

You can easily judge the character of a man by how he treats those who can do nothing for him.

Johann Wolfgang von Goethe

It seems pretty basic, like something we have read in old fairy tales, but still a good quotation about discovering and evaluating character. We might read a fairy tale about a princess who is accustomed to having people do things for her; she meets an angry and filthy traveler limping along on the road between the kingdoms. Instead of acting snobbish and cold, the princess is friendly and offers to help the traveler, even though the traveler cannot give the princess anything.

In the fairy tale, this is often a test of character. We discover this fact when the traveler reveals herself to be a wizard, witch, or magical fairy working for the king of the neighboring kingdom and testing the princess's character in order to marry his son. Of course, the princess passes this test since she was kind and offered to help the traveler, even though she wouldn't gain anything by helping.

How you treat everyone says something about your character. So remember to be open to helping others when you can.

Be true to your work, your word, and your friend.

Henry David Thoreau

Good advice. You can't go wrong with staying true and following this advice. You will have your personal integrity intact. A life lived with integrity is a rich life.

**Conquer yourself
rather than the world.**

Rene Descartes

**The first and the best victory
is to conquer self.**

Plato

Learn how to handle frustration and disappointment. "Conquer" your old response to those feelings. Learn to self-soothe. Learn to breathe your way to center so that you don't snap at others or expect them to soothe you. You are your own healing balm, your own security blanket when you connect to your center, your heart.

**It's not what happens to you,
but how you react to it that matters.**

Epictetus

**What happens is not as important as
how you react to what happens.**

Ellen Glasgow

Your reaction when something negative happens to you demonstrates a lot about your character – about who you are – so try to cultivate a calm response. It is important how you react. Take a breath. Then respond.

On the rollercoaster that is life, you will experience many ups and downs. Realize that you have the power to decide how much you will enjoy the ride.

refresh
examine
refocus

Chapter 4

PERSPECTIVE

and Perception

Perspective. What do you see when you look at a situation or an image? Perhaps you have seen a drawing that looks like a young woman turning her face to her right, or, depending on how you look at it, an old woman. Maybe you have seen a print by MC Escher of birds flying and noticed that there are white birds flying in one direction or black birds flying in the other direction, depending on how you are looking at the image. Escher's prints are famous for how he challenges perspective.

How we look at something changes everything! Our perspective defines what we see and influences how we think and feel about it. Our perspective influences our perception.

**You, yourself, are your own obstacle.
Rise above yourself.**

Hafiz

If someone said this to you when you were sharing a struggle you are having, you might just end the conversation as quickly as you could. I mean, really! It doesn't seem very nurturing or supportive, does it? Yet, after some reflection, you might see Hafiz's wisdom. He alerts us to the fact that we often get in our own way, that we are our own obstacle.

Sometimes our temper creates an obstacle in a relationship. Sometimes our fears, doubts, and anxieties create an obstacle and hold us back when we are thinking of reaching for a goal. And, let's face it, we all feel stuck sometimes.

I love the second half of the quotation because when I read, "rise above yourself," I think of gaining a new perspective, not simply conquering a bad habit or setting aside an old fear. I'm excited by the notion of gaining a new perspective. And you should be too, because when you can see yourself or a situation from up above, you can see so many possibilities. Gaining a new perspective is key to getting out of your own way, to getting "unstuck."

You have both challenges and gifts. What would you be able to do if you weren't holding yourself back? Looking at yourself from a new perspective can help you to soar.

**It's amazing how lovely
common things become, if one only
knows how to look at them.**

Louisa May Alcott

It's all how you look at it, isn't it? We can see ordinary things as beautiful, or as just ordinary, if only we know how to look at them.

For a long time, I thought my older home was not beautiful, because we were always in the middle of fixing it up. One day, I picked up my phone and took some pictures of a few rooms in my house. I was surprised at how lovely the rooms looked, despite the fact that we had not yet refinished the original maple and oak floors and we still had a mixed jumble of furniture. If you know how to look at it, even our furniture could be described as having an eclectic style!

It was really my mood and my belief that things needed to be "picture perfect" in order to be beautiful that kept me from seeing the loveliness of these common things.

I invite you to change your perspective and look at some common things in a different way today. You will be amazed at the beauty you see.

**A boundary is not that at which
something stops, but that from which
something begins.**

Martin Heidegger

Boundaries keep things out and also keep things in, depending on your perspective. A fence marks the end of one person's property and marks the beginning of another.

Endings also mark beginnings. Graduation marks the end of your school years and the beginning of the next chapter of your life. Death marks an ending and a beginning. Depending on your spiritual beliefs, death marks the beginning of an afterlife. For those who remain to mourn the one who died, death marks the beginning of a chapter of life without that person being physically present. It marks the beginning of living with the *memory* of their loved one, rather than their physical being.

Perspective. Each time you complete a chapter of your life, you begin a new one.

**Your mind will give back
exactly what you put into it.**

James Joyce

I thought of a computer program when I read this because a program will only run the way it is set up to run. Input determines output.

When we look at this in terms of living our lives, there is such wisdom in examining our minds. Ask yourself: Exactly what are you programming yourself to feel? How are you programming yourself to respond to the world? Are those programs serving your best interests? If not, then look into ways to change that programming.

**We loiter in winter
while it is already spring.**

Henry David Thoreau

Sometimes we keep ourselves feeling low even after whatever prompted our sadness has passed. Gently remind yourself not to remain stuck in despair or sadness, look out the window and see the winter has passed. Invite happiness in.

Real difficulties can be overcome, it is only the imaginary ones that are unconquerable.

Theodore N. Vail

If you have a leaky faucet or some chipped paint on the wall, you can fix those problems. These difficulties exist in the physical world and have physical solutions. The only difficulties that we can't conquer are those that we imagine to be there: all of our fears and anxieties fall into this category. They are a matter of perception because we perceive a situation a certain way and those perceptions can trigger anxiety.

What if I faint when I stand up to make my speech? What if I am stumped by a question in a job interview? What if I go to an event and no one talks to me? You can't solve a problem that has not happened. What you can do is take some time to acknowledge and address your anxieties or concerns.

Take some time by yourself or get a friend to help you

think through these nerve-wracking imaginings of your mind. You'll find that facing your concerns and addressing them will make them disappear. Because you addressed your fear ahead of time, you won't faint when you go to make that speech. You don't have to solve the problem of fainting, because it didn't actually happen.

Not one of the "what if" scenarios actually happened. They lived only in your imagination. You don't need to resolve difficulties that have not happened, you only need to resolve difficulties that actually happen. You can reduce the number of difficulties that actually happen if you address your imaginary ones ahead of time.

What are the imaginary difficulties that you feel are not conquerable?

**We can complain because
rose bushes have thorns or rejoice
because thorn bushes have roses.**

Abraham Lincoln

Perspective is key when we are complaining about something, isn't it? I smiled when I read this quotation by President Lincoln because I never thought about a rose bush from this perspective! I love roses and do not enjoy dealing with the thorns. It makes me irritated sometimes. If I shift my focus, I can be grateful for the roses without thinking so much about the thorns.

Are there people or situations in your life that you think of as thorns? Can you shift your focus to be grateful for the roses you may find in them?

Very little is needed to make a happy life; it is all within yourself, in your way of thinking.

Marcus Aurelius

How we look at something – a situation, a person, a relationship, a job – affects how we feel about it. Our perspective leads us to our comprehension or understanding and our emotions follow.

Perhaps you've heard the saying: *adopt an attitude of gratitude*. This saying, and this quotation by Marcus Aurelius, are both telling us that if we are looking to find something to be grateful for, we can find it. And when we feel gratefulness, we feel happiness: we have a happy life. At least, we have a happier life than we would if we weren't able to look at life from more than one perspective.

Isn't it great that you have the power to change your perspective each day?

hold on
stay strong
keep going

Chapter 5

PERSISTENCE

Keep on! Persevere! Don't give up! Perseverance is persistence. Some of the many benefits of persistence are meeting your goals and developing a stronger belief in yourself. I hope these quotations will help you persist.

Life is like a cup of tea:
the sugar is all at the bottom!

Julia Ward Howe

What a delightful way to say, "the best is yet to come, keep going!"

If you are a tea drinker, then you know the sugar or the honey often settles down at the bottom of your cup. You can be happily drinking your tea and then you get to the bottom and are surprised to taste that intense sweetness. The rewards of persistence are sweet.

You cannot fail unless you quit.

Abraham Lincoln

I have not failed. I've just found 10,000 ways that won't work.

Thomas A. Edison

I'm sure that you have seen the poster somewhere that defines FAIL as First Attempt In Learning. If you haven't, then now you have; you can keep it in mind if you get discouraged while learning something new.

Edison kept on "failing" until he improved on the incandescent light bulb to the point when it was suitable for home use.

Framing your efforts as failures drains your energy and is discouraging, while re-framing failures into simply one attempt at success energizes and encourages you.

Quitting is an option: failing is not. You can quit one way of doing something until you reach your goal another way. As long as you *persist* in attempting to learn or in attempting to achieve your goal, you have not given up and you have not failed.

I am fond of saying that I love to learn new things, but when learning something new is difficult, I remember that not all learning is fun and easy. Reading fun facts is one thing, learning a new language is something else entirely.

Or how about learning and memorizing a dance routine to be performed on stage before an audience? Not as fun as singing or acting for me, but I did it. I had not been in a musical since I was in college, and there I was in a community theatre production of *Shrek the Musical*, with one daughter in college and the other in high school. For some reason, memorizing a dance routine *was* not, and *is* not, easy for me. It's hard! I was not as confident (read: nervous and discouraged) as the other dancers when learning the steps and the routines. I was a DuLoc Dancer, a Rat Dancer, one of the Three Blind Mice, and the Fairy Godmother. There were dances for each of these roles (Fairy Godmother danced in several numbers) and I did ask to leave the Rat Dancer number. I wanted to quit that one – it was so difficult for me. The director said I could not quit that dance without quitting the entire show. Ugh. So, I did not fail at the exasperatingly difficult Rat Dance. I kept at it until I knew I would not be too embarrassed on the opening night of *Shrek*. I was relieved the lighting for the dance number was low and that I was in the back row of the Rat Dancers. I did the dance. But I was not good at it, and I wished I didn't have to do it. I'm glad to say that I did it, though I will never say yes to being a Rat Dancer again.

I'll take that First Attempt In Learning concept and having persistence any day over giving up and labeling my best efforts as failures. You can too.

**Falling down is not a failure.
Failure comes when you stay where
you have fallen.**

Socrates

In my life, I have taken risks and kept my face toward change and I must say that although I didn't enjoy taking the risks, I loved the results. Auditioning for the school musical my first year and not getting in was tough (actually, I was mortified and felt humiliated by the older students in the room because I was so nervous). But I loved to sing, so I sang to myself in the woods near my house after school each day for an entire year and auditioned again the next year. I got the lead role in *The Sound of Music*! My favorite musical and I was selected to play Maria.

I got up after I fell, even though it took me a year to recover. Falling down is not failure, even though it feels terrible. Don't stay where you are fallen, rise up and show the world what you have to share.

**Don't judge each day
by the harvest you reap but by the
seeds that you plant.**

Robert Louis Stevenson

We won't always see immediate results. Don't get discouraged! Life asks you to see the world as a gardener, not only one who tends to green beans or peas, but as someone who plants oak trees. You have to wait a long time to see the oak tree grow tall.

Focus on the seeds you plant and judge yourself on your efforts, not on the results. If you keep planting and tending the plants, they will grow. Some may not thrive but if you stay focused on planting the seeds then you do not have to worry about not having planted enough. You will have reached your goal.

When I was in my twenties, I interviewed a wise woman who runs a local homeless shelter for a college assignment. I still remember what she said: *Don't worry about the outcome; we cannot worry about the outcome of our efforts, only focus on your efforts. Focus on your efforts and let God worry about the outcome.* I remember thinking that her perspective was wonderful. As a young college student, her statement changed me. I was free. I didn't have to worry so much about the outcome of everything. I saw the wisdom in it too: if you focus on the efforts that you are putting IN, then what comes OUT will likely lead you to your goals and dreams.

**Every step we take on earth
brings us to a new world.**

Federico García Lorca

Every step we take brings us closer to where we are going. Each step we take gives us a different perspective. Both persistence and perspective are important in your journey.

Never give up. No one knows what's going to happen next.

L. Frank Baum

I loved to watch the movie, *The Wizard of Oz* when I was a child. It was so exciting! When it was new to me, I did not know what would happen to Dorothy next. Even when I was scared by the flying monkeys, I didn't want to quit watching just because I was feeling a little nervous. I wanted to keep on watching, I wanted to know what happened next.

If you are trying to solve a problem or achieve a goal, tell yourself not to quit or give up – maybe you'll find the solution in the next minute or hour. Persistence is your friend. Believe and persist.

Remember to look at the flip side of the coin though. When you feel like giving up, listen to your gut. (Or, listen to your inner voice.) You will know if you should walk away because it is not a good fit for you, versus if you were just thinking of giving up because you didn't believe in yourself – two very different situations.

Success is a fruit of slow growth.

Henry Fielding

The fruit of our labors is what we focus on but we need to remember that it takes time for fruit to grow. Sometimes we get frustrated because results don't come fast enough. Persistence is key, especially when we do not see the results of our efforts immediately.

Keep on in your efforts, tend the garden and don't be dismayed if you cannot see the growth. You'll see your success just as surely as cherries follow cherry blossoms.

Doing little things well is a step toward doing big things better.

Vincent van Gogh

Van Gogh gives good advice to keep going when we don't see the big results that we'd like. Focus on doing what you can as well as you can. Do not stop to evaluate or judge yourself or your results as not being "enough." Think of Van Gogh learning to draw, learning to paint, learning about different perspectives and Impressionism and coming up with a style that he was eventually praised for; he did the little things well and got better at them and went on to do big things better. He went from small charcoal sketches to great oil paintings.

This quotation sound like a mom said it to her child, doesn't it? I like how gentle and encouraging it sounds. I hope that it encourages you today.

You are enough. Just for today, do the little things well and know that this is enough.

look within
gratitude
compassion

Chapter 6

HAPPINESS

Everyone wants to be happy. Finding happiness is not a destination, it is a journey. Our journey is made up of a series of choices that create a domino effect:

> • the choices we make determine the outcome of our journey
> • the outcome of our journey determines the quality of our life
> • the quality of our life determines the quality of our happiness

Happiness is a choice; the choice to be happy is a choice to be present. The choice to be present is a choice to be grateful. The choice to be grateful is a choice to be kind. The choice to be kind is a choice to be loving. These choices depend on your thoughts and perspective as much as your actual circumstances.

Where is happiness? So often people speak of "seeking" happiness and "finding" happiness, but we cannot seek happiness from an external source. It is within ourselves.

**Someone once asked me
what I regarded as the three most
important requirements for happiness.
My answer was: A feeling that you
have been honest with yourself and
those around you; a feeling that you
have done the best you could both in
your personal life and in your work;
and the ability to love others.**

Eleanor Roosevelt

Do you have your own three most important requirements for happiness? Sounds like something for a
New Year's resolution yet it's worth examining.

I think that Eleanor Roosevelt nailed it. "*A feeling that
you have been honest….*" Being honest with yourself:
huge. Being honest with those around you: yep, also
right up there as fundamental to your self-esteem and
well-being (you know you are okay when your personal integrity is intact). Not easy, but honesty is your
foundation, it is your rock. Rocks are hard but they
also give you great support beneath your feet if they

are large, placed well, and smooth from years of walking and standing on.

"A feeling that you have done the best you could...." Yes! You will feel happy with yourself if you feel that you have done the best you could in your work and your personal life.

"...and the ability to love others." The ability to love others in an honest way filled with personal integrity will bring you great joy. I believe that she is referring to the kind of love that is healthy, and this kind of ability to love comes from working on yourself and your issues (whatever they may be, and we all have them). When you have met and managed your issues (your obstacles in your ability to love), you have a great ability to love others. When you love others and welcome them into your life, joy and happiness are yours.

Today, gently invite your heart to: be honest, do your best, and love others.

> **Happiness is like a butterfly; the more you chase it, the more it will elude you, but if you turn your attention to other things, it will come and sit softly on your shoulder.**

Henry David Thoreau

Contentment comes to my mind when I think of happiness like this butterfly. So soft and gentle, the butterfly lands. This notion of happiness seems so Zen-like to me and I'm sure that more than one person has expressed it similarly. Yet, the sheer gentle joy of it makes it worth repeating. Turn your thoughts and efforts to what your personal integrity guides you to do and focus on that, not on how much happiness you think is eluding you.

When you are not desperately seeking it, and you are focused on living your best, most intentional and authentic life, then happiness will softly sit in your heart and radiate outward to others.

Happiness will never come to those who fail to appreciate what they already have.

Buddha

One way to read this is that happiness will *come to you* when you appreciate what you have already.

If we want to experience more happiness, then we can cultivate a grateful heart for the incredible things that are already in our lives right now. I know that this might sound preachy and difficult, but there are ways to develop gratitude. We can shift our focus: focus on what good came out of a bad situation, focus on what lessons you may have learned.

Adopt an attitude of gratitude. This action is which similar to shifting our focus because it is really about how we are taking in information. A therapist once told me that people sometimes view a bad situation through their feelings and thus, "awfulized" it, defined it as worse than it was. If we can remove some of the intense feelings from our perceptions, then we can respond with less negative thoughts and can begin to see the neutral and then the good.

When we can see the good, we are on our way to seeing what there is to be grateful for in a given situation. And a grateful heart produces happiness.

If you want others to be happy, practice compassion. If you want to be happy, practice compassion.

Dalai Lama

When we are compassionate, we want to relieve or remove and soothe another person's distress. We put ourselves in the other person's place without judging and try to help. We try to help in difficult situations, we try to be a sympathetic listener. We value how other people feel. We remove angry and aggressive behavior in our approach. We work toward a peaceful and pleasant atmosphere at work and at home.

When we practice compassion, we build relationships that are more genuine and authentic: we connect on a deeper level with people.

We also practice self-compassion. All those ways we practice compassion with others, we also practice with ourselves.

Showing kindness to ourselves and to others is a good feeling – it makes us happy. If you want to be happy, practice compassion.

Happiness often sneaks in through a door you didn't know you left open.

John Barrymore

Has happiness crept up on you and surprised you?

Even when we're feeling sad, we might have left an opening for happiness. Happiness can unexpectedly greet you. Today, reflect on being open, and opening your heart.

The happiness of your life depends upon the quality of your thoughts.

Marcus Aurelius

Reflect on the quality of your daily thoughts for a moment. How do you talk to yourself? Are most of your thoughts negative and stressful, or do you have so many positive thoughts that you barely notice the things that don't go as planned (go wrong) each day? Perhaps you are in the middle, not dwelling on the negative, but not walking on clouds either. No matter where your thoughts are, they are having a huge impact on how you feel because our thoughts spark emotional and physical responses.

Notice that once your train of thought gets going in one direction, it tends to pick up speed and remain on that track. In order change tracks, we must make a conscious effort to turn our thoughts in another direction. Go ahead and acknowledge what you are feeling, and then think about the triggering situation from as many other perspectives as you can so that you don't remain stuck in your initial response. Often it feels good to go through this process with a friend, but you can do it by yourself too.

Use your happy thoughts to create a happy life.

Happiness is when what you think, what you say, and what you do are in harmony.

Mahatma Gandhi

Gandhi frames happiness in our own personal integrity. Even as I'm writing this, I feel a profound sense of what is at the center of human happiness. I feel grounded in this wisdom that directs each of us to our center, to our personal integrity which is our core.

When what you think, what you say, and what you do are aligned and sent forth into the world, then you are expressing the best of who you are.

You are creating who you are each time you think, say, or do anything. So, when your thoughts, your words, and your deeds are all in harmony, you are saying what you mean and following through on your word by doing what you said you would do.

It feels wonderful when we follow through and keep

our promises to ourselves and to others. And this harmony is happiness.

If one thinks that one is happy, that is enough to be happy.

Madame de LaFayette

Your thoughts determine your emotions. Dwell on happy thoughts more often than sad ones, if at all possible. Train yourself not to stay stuck in despair by changing your behavior when you're struggling. Reach out more often to friends, practice self-care, read a book, take a walk, watch a movie. Notice your thoughts and steer them toward a perspective that moves you from stuck to hopeful and on your way to happy. Your happiness and your thoughts are related.

In real life and in fiction, you are happier when your thoughts are happier. In *Peter Pan*, Wendy, John and Michael could fly with the help of a little pixie dust and "lovely thoughts," and in the Harry Potter books, Harry used a strong happy memory to create a Patronus that protected him from harm. Though you are not a character in a children's story, you can gently guide yourself toward more constructive, healthy, and nurturing self-talk and thoughts each day.

You are in charge of your thoughts. You have great freedom and power to entertain any thoughts you wish. Isn't that a great feeling? It makes me happy just to think about it.

know yourself
trust yourself
accept yourself

Chapter 7

BELIEVE IN YOURSELF

Believe in yourself and your abilities, and you will be amazed at what you can achieve. These quotations are here to inspire you to keep believing.

Believe in yourself,
even when no one else does.

Anonymous

Always believe in yourself. What others think of you does not define you. You define yourself. Keep strong in your belief in yourself, even when those around you doubt you. You know who you are.

As soon as you trust yourself,
you will know how to live.

Johann Wolfgang von Goethe

In terms of importance, trusting yourself is right up there with believing in yourself.

How do you develop trust in yourself? The same way you developed trust in others. You have experience and a track record with yourself just the same way you do with family, friends, and coworkers. The more times that you keep your word to yourself, the more that you will trust that you will keep your promises to yourself.

As with any character trait or good habit, you practice until it becomes part of you. When you trust yourself, you will know in what areas you can depend on yourself to accomplish something, such as writing a report or a speech, or always being available to give your friend a ride to a dentist appointment. You'll also know in what areas you can trust that you won't be able to do something and you will set limits, boundaries, and define yourself. Maybe you are better at researching than writing and you work with a coworker on that report, maybe you have a demanding job so you will only drive that friend to some appointments, but not every time they need a ride somewhere.

Whatever the situation might be, it is true that as soon as you trust yourself, you'll know how to live. Knowing yourself and trusting yourself is a good feeling.

A very little key will open a very heavy door.

Charles Dickens

If you can believe in yourself, even a little, then you can do great things. You don't need absolute certainty that you can achieve perfection before you can begin a project. All you need is a small amount of belief or confidence, a spark, and you can begin a large project or an intimidating activity.

How wonderful that this notion of the small key opening the large door is true in the physical world as well as in the mind's ability to motivate us! When you think of a small key unlocking a very large and heavy door, you can imagine that the task at hand is achievable as long as you don't think your way into being completely discouraged.

Even if you have some doubts about completing a monumental task, you can think of a very small key, and smile, and know that you have enough belief in yourself to begin.

**One who believes in himself
has no need to convince others.**

Laozi

When you believe in yourself, you feel confident and calm and you just know that you are worthy so you don't feel the need to make sure that others know how wonderful you are. Since you are wonderful and loving, they will see your worth and they will see that you believe in yourself.

**Do not judge yourself harshly.
Without mercy for ourselves we
cannot love the world.**

Buddha

Believing in yourself means loving yourself. I know from personal experience that it is easy to judge yourself harshly while still loving others, but there is even more love available when we reduce our self-judgement. There is even more mercy for others once we heal ourselves and forgive our own shortcomings.

Love yourself, and you will find that you love the world.

The future belongs to those who believe in the beauty of their dreams.

Eleanor Roosevelt

How many times have you been told to believe in your dreams? Many, I'll bet. Yet, it is good advice. If you believe in your dreams, then you will take action to make them come true.

Holding on to the vision, the beauty of your dreams will motivate you. So, I think that Eleanor Roosevelt was definitely on to something here. She certainly believed in the beauty of her dreams of equality for all people and she achieved so much in her lifetime.

**You yourself, as much as
anybody in the entire universe,
deserve your love and affection.**

Buddha

A favorite quotation, and one to come back to when
feeling down or discouraged. The notion of treating
yourself as you would treat your best friend or your
favorite family member is not new, but it is one to be
revisited often. Believe that you are as lovable as anyone you know.

You deserve love. Believe that you deserve love. You
deserve the kind of love that you give to the person or
animal that you cherish the most. Be gentle and kind
and loving to yourself each day. You deserve your
love and affection.

**Optimism is the faith that
leads to achievement. Nothing can be
done without hope and confidence.**

Helen Keller

Confidence, hope, faith, optimism, each of these terms
is connected to believing. Believe in yourself. Believe
in your goals. Believe in your dreams. Borrow a little
energy from optimism, faith, hope and the confidence
you feel and turn your mind to a belief unshakable.

**You can be pleased with nothing
if you are not pleased with yourself.**

Mary Wortley Montagu

Fundamentally, you need to be pleased with yourself. It is your foundation for everything else. This doesn't mean that you won't ever be discouraged! You will. Yet, when your base is solid, you have the ability to anchor yourself, ground yourself, plant yourself. You are buffeted about far less when you are planted on solid ground than you are when you do not have that ground beneath you. That ground is your love for yourself. When you believe in yourself, you will find you are pleased with yourself.

When you are not pleased with yourself, you can feel that the entire world is annoying, and you might be snapping at people more and find yourself being defensive more than you usually are.

You can be pleased with yourself on a consistent basis

when you regularly tend to *your relationship with your-self*: take time to respect, understand, accept, and appreciate yourself and you will be pleased with yourself.

Nothing is more intolerable
than to have admit to yourself
your own errors.

Ludwig van Beethoven

I can see why Beethoven said this; I am often irritated with myself when I make a mistake. Who isn't?
Oh, there are some of you out there that are much more Zen than I am, I forgot. And I love that you are!

What I also see in this quotation is that nothing is more *freeing* than acknowledging that I am not perfect. I feel light and free when I admit mistakes as I make them. I am released from torment.

Believe that you are worthy, no matter how many errors you make.

listen with
tolerance
speak truth

Chapter 8

COMMUNICATION

and Your Heart

Communication gets complicated. Uncomplicate
it when you can. Speak from the heart and listen
through your heart.

Never apologize for showing feeling. When you do so, you apologize for the truth.

Benjamin Disraeli

Showing how you feel is part of communication. Your gestures, your facial expressions and your voice covey what you think and feel. Your affection, your distaste, your passion, your disinterest, your excitement, your boredom are all expressions of how you're feeling.

Whether you are moved to exclaim your joy, or your voice trembles while holding back tears, you are communicating your feelings and there is no lie and no shame in expressing them. Feelings are true – and you don't need to apologize for showing them.

Dogs are better than human beings because they know but do not tell.

Emily Dickinson

Dogs know, but they do not tell. People, not so much. People love to gossip. Not everyone tells all, but often the line is blurry. What should we share with others? What shouldn't we share?

Dogs are loyal. People are loyal too. As people develop their character, they develop more mature behaviors; loyalty and discretion are traits people develop to greater and lesser degrees. Your loyalty and understanding of how to be discreet will lead you to be a good friend – maybe even as good as Man's Best Friend. But Emily Dickinson would still trust a dog before she would trust a human.

Today, think a while about trust, loyalty, and keeping some things to yourself.

Silence is the best response to a fool.

Elizabeth Barrett Browning

You do not have to engage in a conversation or debate with everyone who initiates one. Choose to spend your time and energy wisely. People can make statements just to provoke others. They think it is fun. Unless you enjoy a form of conversation that is like a dog chasing its tail, silence is the best response to a fool.

No amount of evidence will ever persuade an idiot.

Mark Twain

Have you ever regretted getting into an argument that was more of a debate? Did you regret it because the person holding the opposite viewpoint would not see your evidence as relevant and accurate?

Sometimes, no amount of evidence will persuade someone that your statement or claim is factual because that person just says that your evidence is not valid.

I'm in favor of asking questions about evidence, of testing evidence to make sure that it is accurate and relevant. Be warned: not everyone cares about evaluating the evidence. Some don't know that standard tests of evidence in speech exist. They may also use fallacies (faulty reasoning) when explaining or defending their position without realizing it.

Someone is ignorant if they are unaware of the evidence or of the ways to determine if the evidence is valid. Someone is an idiot if they don't even try to cure their ignorance. They will never be persuaded by your evidence because they don't want to examine it or all sides of the issue.

What to do? Ignorant people can be worth debating if they are open to learning more. You may be ignorant, too, of some points on the other side of the debate.

Idiots? Don't waste your breath on someone who doesn't want to listen. Save your energy for people who genuinely want to understand your position.

**Listen with ears of tolerance!
See through the eyes of compassion!
Speak with the language of love.**

Rumi

Communication involves input and output. If your input is filtered through tolerance and compassion, then your output will be sprinkled with love. When your language is loving, then you are well on your way to being the best version of yourself and living an amazing life filled with love.

**Everything you say should be true,
but not everything true should be said.**

Voltaire

This quotation reminds me of the Emily Dickinson quotation about dogs being better than humans because they know but they do not tell, with a twist: everything you say should be true.

Honest communication is key to our relationships and part of our personal integrity. Take some time to think about if everything you say is truthful; take even more time to think about whether or not you should say it.

What comes from the heart goes to the heart.

Samuel Taylor Coleridge

Did you ever get goosebumps when you were listening to someone speak? Or when you were saying something that was really important to you? Then you know that when someone is passionate about a cause, or feeling tender and affectionate, their message is coming from their heart. Their words affect you deeply because what comes from the heart, does indeed go straight into our hearts.

What does your heart want to say today? Is there an unspoken message waiting there for you to share it? Your heart will help you connect with so many others – if you let it speak.

Never trust your tongue
when your heart is bitter.

Samuel Johnson

When we are feeling bitterness and anger, we are likely to say something we'll regret later. Give yourself time to calm down, to regroup before you say something. I'm reminded of a Scottish proverb: "Give your tongue more holidays than your head." Of course, it means to think before you speak and to think more than you speak, but it also applies to speaking when you are angry or bitter too.

Don't trust your tongue when you are bitter, give it a holiday instead.

**To get closer to Truth and Right,
we need a beautiful and soft heart.**

Shams Tabrizi

A beautiful and soft heart is a heart that is open. A heart that is open listens. Listening is the path to Truth and Right.

love of self
kindness
imperfection

Chapter 9

LOVE & FORGIVENESS

Love is more than simple affection. Love is kindness. Love is forgiveness. Love is also found in our strength to treat others with compassion, even when we are having a bad day and are short-tempered. Love is love of humanity and love of self, for we cannot love others well if we do not love ourselves first.

Who loves a lot, forgives a lot.

Amado Nervo

When you love yourself, when you love others, you spend a lot of time forgiving yourself, and a lot of time forgiving those you love. This is the nature of love and human nature.

When you are in a relationship – even a relationship with yourself – you will find that you and your loved ones make mistakes and you will need to forgive yourself and the other person. The more intimate the relationship is, the more you will discover the need for forgiveness. We are all imperfect and we'll encounter differences and misunderstandings that will need smoothing and forgiveness and love. Forgiving is a part of love: forgiveness *is* love.

**Have a heart that never hardens,
and a temper that never tires,
and a touch that never hurts.**

Charles Dickens

Love is a verb. Keep acting with a loving heart and keep smoothing the rough edges of your temperament.

Stay centered in love, in your heart, and act from there. Love yourself. Love others.

**A man would do nothing
if he waited until he could do it so well
that no one could find fault.**

John Henry Newman

Oh, to never make a mistake! But if you wait to do something so well that everyone thinks it is perfect, then you won't do anything at all. You'll be paralyzed with the fear of not being perfect. You won't even be able to begin a task.

This quotation speaks to overcoming perfectionism. How can we resist being ensnared by perfectionism? Through self-love.

None of us is perfect. We are wonderfully human and we each do things a little differently than anyone else. I know that the world expects you to be perfect and you expect yourself to be perfect. Don't give in to that warped way of thinking. Love yourself for being your imperfect self.

It takes courage and a love of self to show others that we are not perfect, but only when we are known for who we really are will we feel accepted and truly loved. The book, *The Velveteen Rabbit* talks about being Real, and that means showing the world your real self that is not perfect. It is important to be Real, "... because once you are Real you can't be ugly, except to people who don't understand."

Once you are real – and not perfect – you can't be anything but beautiful to those who know you and love you.

Be kind, for everyone you meet is fighting a difficult battle.

Plato

A great reminder to treat others with compassion. You have no idea what people are going through; you simply do not know the struggles each person is facing.

Respond to others with kindness as often as you can.

It is very unfair to judge of anybody's conduct, without an intimate knowledge of their situation.

Jane Austen

Love more, judge less. Judge less, love more.

**Holding on to anger is like
grasping a hot coal with the intent
of throwing it at someone else;
you are the one who gets burned.**

Buddha

Have you heard this one? Wise, isn't it? When we
hold on to anger, we are unable to access forgiveness.
When we are angry and unforgiving, we are not loving.

Resist the temptation to hold on to your anger; you
are hurting yourself the most. Release the anger and
move toward forgiveness. Forgiveness will lead you
to love.

The best portion of a good man's life: his little, nameless unremembered acts of kindness and love.

William Wordsworth

Nameless unremembered acts of kindness and love are the best part of life. I mentioned "random acts of kindness," in another chapter of this book, and it looks like Wordsworth knew this long before it was trending in the 1990s. You can do little things for people that will mean a lot to them, like paying for someone's washing or drying at a laundry mat, or feeding quarters into someone's parking meter (yes, they still exist!).

A really great person is the person who makes every person feel great.

G.K. Chesterton

I hope that you can think of more than one person you have met who makes every person feel great. Some people just make everyone feel wonderful! They make you feel loved. You don't even notice at the time that it is love. But it is, it's love.

I've been lucky to know several teachers, coaches, friends, and family members who have made me feel great, made me feel loved. My high school drama teacher and speech team coach, Mr. Fretland, was one of these great people. He made each of his students feel special and loved. We thought of ourselves as "Fret's kids," and still gather for a Fret reunion each summer.

How do these people make you feel great? And how do you know that it is love? Because these people treat you with respect: they don't talk down to you, they validate you and your feelings. They will be at your side if you need them when you feel sad or discouraged.

They have personal integrity and see your integrity and your strength of character. They see your strengths and they challenge you to do more. They laugh with you; they break out into a huge grin when they see you. They build up your confidence; they show enthusiasm for you and your efforts.

A really great person makes you feel really great because they see you, they know you, and they love you.

**Kindness is the language
which the deaf can hear and
the blind can see.**

Mark Twain

Kindness and love are universally understood. We all understand a hug.

change
your course
spread your
light

Chapter 10

WRAPPING UP YOUR HEART

These gems inspired me, or made me laugh, or made me think. They touch on trusting your own advice, focusing on continuous improvement rather than perfection, not worrying too much, changing your course, spreading your light, and rethinking normal. I hope these pages speak to your head and your heart.

Be the sun and all will see you.

Fyodor Dostoevsky

Summon your confidence and don't be afraid to be the sun. You are the sun! Your warmth and light will be happily received when you let yourself be known as the sun that you are.

Cast fear and doubt aside and let your light shine. All will see you. Don't be afraid to be seen. Many people are waiting for your warmth and light. Go. Shine.

Normality is a paved road: It's comfortable to walk, but no flowers grow on it.

Vincent van Gogh

"Normal," means doing something in a conventional way – the way something has always been done – or following the rules. Some rules are necessary, of course. Having conventions and norms for behaviors help society to run smoothly. For example, you should not falsely shout, "Fire," in a crowded movie theater because this convention keeps us safe. Or, we all know that we need to wait our turn in line at a store or an event.

These examples of normality are not what Van Gogh is referring to. What we are taught as *normal* behavior can be stifling. We are so often taught to be quiet when we are taught about normal behavior. Is normality what you are going for? Looking to fit in so that you won't feel uncomfortable?

Normal is boring.

It feels safe and comfortable to conform to the norms of those around us; but when we silence ourselves for the sake of fitting in, we lose an opportunity to become known and accepted for who we are. Think of how children behave when they don't know what "normal," behavior is: they talk loudly; they ask questions in public spaces without considering whether or not they know the person; they sing in public. They are free to express themselves and become known and accepted and *appreciated* for who they are.

I remember a time when a few of my young nieces sang, "Take Me Out to the Ball Game," in its entirety on a public bus filled with people on their way to the state fair. The passengers applauded after the song was finished.

Those young girls were not silenced by the normal rules of behavior when riding the bus. It was an opportunity to become known, accepted, and appreciated for who they were as unique individuals.

These are the flowers that grow on the unpaved path – the path that is not paved with "normal" behavior.

It takes courage to sing on the bus! It's brave! Not all of us want to sing on the bus, but there are other risks we can take that will yield flowers.

Throw off your worries when you throw off your clothes at night.

Napoleon Bonaparte

I don't exactly "throw" off my clothes at night, but I can see the energy that those words give to throwing off your worries. It sounds much more freeing than simply *setting aside* your worries.

You are wise to throw off your worries at night because you are giving yourself much needed balance between contemplating your concerns during the day and recharging yourself with stress-free sleep. You balance a time to relax with time tending to the worries of the day.

So, cast them off! Your worries, that is. You can do what you want with your clothes.

Nobody can give you wiser advice than yourself.

Marcus Tullius Cicero

Have you ever asked a friend for advice and not followed it? I have. What happens is, as soon as I hear the other person's view of what I should do, my heart tells me what I should do. It's as if I just need to hear the various viewpoints out loud and then I know what I want to do, how I want to proceed. I guess that I know myself better than anyone else knows me. Trust your gut. Trust your heart.

You are your own best friend and you give great advice. Follow it.

There are two ways of spreading light: to be the candle or the mirror that reflects it.

Edith Wharton

Sometimes you are the candle, spreading your light and your joy, sometimes you are the mirror. A friend, a sister, a daughter may be the candle: she is shining and you are reflecting her love, her luminous joy. Each of us has times when it is our turn to shine and times when it is our turn to support someone else.

The mirror is as important as the candle; it increases the amount of light we see from the candle.

Open up and spread the light of your heart. Be the candle. Be the mirror. Keep shining and help others to shine more brightly every chance you get.

Don't feel sorry for yourself if you have chosen the wrong road; turn around.

Edgar Cayce

If you find yourself in a situation where you are sad and maybe frustrated and discouraged or feeling like you made the wrong choice, then stop. You can change course.

Many people in history have changed course. Vincent van Gogh traveled down more than one career path before he found the one that gave him the most happiness and success (even though that success was after his death).

Vincent van Gogh was an art dealer, then he was also a Protestant missionary. He cared so much about the people he ministered to that he alarmed them: he didn't dress or act like other missionaries did. He gave everything away – his food and his clothes.

After drifting for a while, he found something he could do that gave him happiness and purpose in the last ten years of his life, despite his poor physical and mental health. With financial support from his brother Theo, Van Gogh was able to spend the rest of his life learning, drawing, and painting.

Van Gogh found his purpose and you can too. If you don't like the direction you're going; turn around and go down a different path.

Continuous improvement is better than delayed perfection.

Mark Twain

Take one small, imperfect step each day and you will reach your destination sooner than if you wait until each step is perfectly executed.

The beginning is always today.

Mary Wollstonecraft Shelley

Today is the best time to begin something. Actually, it is the *only* time to begin something. This quotation reminds us that we only have the present: yesterday is done and tomorrow has not begun. The present moment is all we have.

What did you think of when you read this quotation? Is there something you'd like to begin?

Maybe you'll start something today that is a beginning of a project or relationship that you'll still be involved with ten years from now. You never know what you'll do today that will be the start of something that will endure for years. Mighty oaks from little acorns grow. What you do each day counts. Each day, you create the foundation for your tomorrow.

EPILOGUE

Here are two favorite quotations to keep close to you. My mom has both of these on the mirror in her bathroom so she can see them each day. I also have copies of them. And now you do too.

Finish each day and be done with it.
You have done what you could.
Some blunders and absurdities
no doubt crept in;
Forget them as soon as you can.
Tomorrow is a new day;
You shall begin it serenely,
And with too high a spirit
To be encumbered
with your old nonsense.

Ralph Waldo Emerson

Look to this day:
For it is life, the very life of life.
In its brief course
Lie all the verities and realities
of your existence:
The bliss of growth,
The glory of action,
The splendor of beauty.

For yesterday is but a dream
And tomorrow is only a vision;
But today, well-lived, makes every
Yesterday a dream of happiness
And every tomorrow a vision of hope.
Look well, therefore, to this day!

Sanskrit Poem
LOOK TO THIS DAY